The Ri:

JOHN G. GREENSHIELDS

Copyright © 2023 John G. Greenshields
All rights reserved.

ISBN: 9798870114057

DEDICATION

To the churches who have journeyed through Advent with me over the years; to my loving family who have encouraged me in writing this; and most of all to Jesus, whose advent we celebrate, my sincere thanks.

CONTENTS

There are no chapter headings. Each day of this devotional guide, indeed each day of our lives, begins a new chapter in our journey with Jesus. May each day be better than the one before!

Cover picture: Sunrise over Puerto Calero harbour, Lanzarote.

Introduction

The season of Advent - a special time for Christians, or a superficial man-made construct? A period of frantic last-minute planning for Christmas, or an opportunity to explore a deeper encounter with the incarnate Lord? Too often it comes and goes, and we skim across the surface rather than plumb the depths. If Jesus' incarnation is the greatest ever miracle, as one New Testament teacher[1] described it, should we not take time to reflect on and engage with this amazing God who took on human flesh in the person of his Son? This devotional guide, moving slowly through Luke 1-2, seeks to help in that quest. Each day has a short reading, with breaks to reflect on some Messianic Psalms each Sunday.

Why Luke? Of all the gospel writers, he has most to share concerning the period before and immediately after the birth of Jesus. As a dearly loved doctor, a man of science and faith who cared about the well-being of others, his unique interest and careful investigations are worth pondering. Where did Luke get his information? Almost certainly from Mary, or someone very close to her. Who else could have offered such access to these detailed and intimate memories of that tumultuous time?

How can you make best use of this guide?
- Use it one day at a time
- Read the Scripture passage slowly
- Pray as you read, asking the Holy Spirit to speak
- For maximum benefit, share this journey with a small group
- Keep focussed on Jesus, the incarnate Son of God
- **Going further...**each day invites you to think about applying what you have read.

---

[1] Rev. R.E.O. White, late Principal of the Baptist Theological College of Scotland, lecturing in 1971.

(Sun)Day 1 - Messianic Psalm 40

Doctor Luke will be our main guide during this Advent journey. Before we turn to his gospel, we go further back in the Bible story to Israel's wonderful songbook found in the book of Psalms. We start with a psalm from Israel's greatest king, David, who penned most of these worship songs.

Messianic Psalms
Advent Sunday begins this journey. We begin with one of the "Messianic Psalms". These emerge from a particular context, but go far beyond, and can be clearly linked with Jesus. For example, Psalm 40 is quoted and applied to him by the writer of Hebrews in chapter 10:5-10. We can never know how much inspired writers like David could actually see in the distant future. Yet their words, arising out of their own times and experiences, provide fascinating prophetic glimpses of what God will do through the incarnation of his Son.

Waiting
Advent is really about two realities found in this psalm - waiting and coming. David's song starts with familiar words "I waited patiently for the Lord". There's a challenge immediately for many of us in those words. Most children can hardly be said to be waiting patiently for Christmas! The very idea of waiting for something is counter-cultural. We order online and confidently expect delivery the next day. Or we send electronic messages conveyed in seconds and complain if there's not an instant reply. King David, the author of Psalm 40, would understand the frustrations that can come through waiting.

We don't know the background to this psalm, although there are some clues. There's trouble and distress (v2, 12), awareness of sin (v12), the need for divine help (v13), danger from enemies (v14), and prayer for deliverance (v17). David's past experience encourages him to trust God in the present (v1-2). He has waited before, and that encourages him to wait patiently for the Lord now. He anticipates that God will act. His waiting will not be in vain. Neither is our waiting if our focus is on the Lord.

The waiting in itself becomes a vital part of prayer, praise, and surrender to God's will and ways. We can wait in miserable self-contemplation, or wait expectantly, looking for his new day dawning.

Coming
Advent literally means "coming". V6-8 reveal David's desire to obey God's will in his life; not through sacrifice, but through obedience. "I have come…to do your will".

Speaking of the sacrifice that takes away sins, it's the writer of Hebrews who takes these words from Psalm 40 and applies them to the Lord Jesus Christ. What David wrote goes far beyond his time and experience, and is now fulfilled in Jesus, who has come to do God's will. His incarnation was and is effective. He did come as promised. Through his obedience, he did accomplish God's will. He offered a sacrifice for our sins acceptable for all time. The waiting was worth it when his coming occurred.

> *The light of Israel*
> *shall become a fire,*
> *and the Holy One a flame,*
> *the child of miracles,*
> *born to be Messiah,*
> *over all the earth to reign*[2]

---

[2] John Pantry, *Rejoice, you sons of Israel*, © 1992 Thankyou Music

Going further...

- The late Eugene Peterson encouraged his readers to approach the Psalms creatively. So read Psalm 40 aloud, pray it, sing it, meditate on it, share it.

- As you do so, give thanks for this time of waiting during Advent to celebrate the coming of the incarnate Lord.

Day 2: Read Luke 1:1-4

Theophilus
In one long Greek sentence, Luke introduces us to his friend Theophilus - "God's friend" or "loved by God". Apart from his name, we know nothing more about him, but thank God for this man to whom Luke addresses his gospel. Now we can read it too! Luke writes to bring reassurance of the truth and strengthen the faith of his friend. Intriguingly he tells us that many had written accounts of these events, while Luke also writes a sequel (Acts).

Luke
Note in Luke's opening words the care with which he delves into his source material. He uses reliable reports and, most importantly, eye-witness accounts. Luke is not a student locked away in a secluded library, but a keen interviewer taking in what he can from those who were there when these things happened. This beloved doctor is simultaneously a good historian. Thorough research underpins his historical accuracy.

God
These events are not only historically reliable. They are also in line with ancient prophecies anticipating the coming of the Messiah. In them a divine plan is being fulfilled. God is bringing to pass what has been predicted long ago. All these things, says Luke, "have been fulfilled among us" (v1). Behind his narrative stands the God whose purpose is being worked out in the story of salvation. The incarnation is both a climax and a fulcrum. It is the fulfilment of a long-expected event, and the pivot of time itself. Christmas carols often capture the deep significance of this. Deceptively simple words mask profound theology.

*See, amid the winter's snow,
born for us on earth below,
see, the Lamb of God appears,
promised from eternal years*[3]

As we journey through Advent, we find assurance in Luke's first words that these events are historically accurate, reliable, and revelatory. Exploring this story, drilling down into it, will deepen our faith and reassure us of the truth taught by his followers since the time of Christ. Luke invites us to explore with him, understand, and believe.

Going further…

- How we can assess the historical reliability of what Luke records?

- Pray for those exploring the story of Jesus, or struggling with doubt. Could you invite them to join you in this Advent journey?

---

[3] Edward Caswall (1814-1878)

Day 3: Read Luke 1:5-7

I still vividly remember our "family doctor" as GPs were once known! When he came to our home, his concern was for the whole family, not just the sick person. Doctor Luke reminds me of him. Before meeting Jesus, we are led into the story of his wider family, in particular Mary's relative Elizabeth and her husband Zechariah; the parents of the man named John, whose birth and life would prepare the way for Jesus.

A childless couple
In the time of King Herod the Great (who reigned 37-4BC), Luke's story begins with a sad situation. Picture an elderly couple, devout and righteous, the husband a priest; his wife also from a priestly family. Blameless, holy, and highly respected, yet their lives blighted by childlessness. And, given their advancing years, little or no prospect of a baby.

Even with modern medical advances, many couples today share the experience of Zechariah and Elizabeth, living with the pain and disappointment of not having children. Emptiness, frustration, apparently fruitless prayers, even social disdain, are all too common for people living with this sad reality. Verse 25 reflects the popular view then that childlessness might well be a sign of God's disfavour.

When we struggle with what life has brought us, how do we react and respond? What can we learn from this elderly couple?

- They continue to worship God, serve him, and live according to his word. They refuse to succumb to bitterness, or allow their disappointment to dominate their lives. Did they realise that bad things happen to good people, and that God's people are not immune?

- They trust God, even when there is no understanding or rational explanation of their frustrated hopes. They are willing for him to have the last word on their situation - and what a word that would be. One Jewish Rabbi makes the point that whenever Scripture says that a woman was childless, later a child is born to her.

- They know that God sees and understands; and as the story unfolds, that he has chosen them for a hugely significant role, even in their older age.

Hopes and fears
The carol "O little town of Bethlehem," written following the author's visit to Israel, vividly depicts hope shining through despair.

> *Yet in your dark streets shining*
> *is everlasting light;*
> *the hopes and fears of all the years*
> *are met in you tonight*[4]

The hopes and fears of Zechariah and Elizabeth are known by God. While others may have seen their situation as his judgement, he has something special in mind for them.

Going further…

- Thank God for people whose godly lives have influenced and helped to shape you.

- What challenges are being faced right now, in your life, or in others you know? In the light of today's reading, how will you pray?

---

[4] Phillips Brooks (1835-93)

Day 4: Read Luke 1:8-10

Zechariah was one of some 18,000 priests who served at the Jerusalem temple. This vast number of men was divided into groups, with daily rotas to cover the whole year. Each priest would serve for two weeks annually, with lots drawn daily to determine who would go into the holy place and burn incense to accompany the sacrificial offering. For the chosen priest, this was the greatest moment of his priestly career, quite literally a once-in-a-lifetime event. Imagine Zechariah's excitement when his name is chosen.

God at work
Zechariah's chances of being picked were 18,000 to 1. Yet God had chosen him and his wife Elizabeth to be part of his plan for the coming of his Son into the world. When Alfred B. Smith and Eugene Clark wrote their hymn "I do not know what lies ahead," the chorus included the words "with God things don't just happen, everything by him is planned[5]." Nothing is random when God is at work. Only Zechariah would be chosen that particular day and time, for God is active in the story of this old priest whose name is picked by chance to go and offer incense in the temple's holy place. God is orchestrating all these events in preparation for the coming of his Son, stirring in hearts longing for him.

Incense and prayer
Throughout Scripture, sacred incense and prayer are linked together. See Revelation 5:8 and 8:3-4. The picture of Zechariah offering incense inside the temple, with the assembled worshippers outside praying, is a potent one. There is a clear sense of something about to happen: when God is at work, one of the manifestations is an increasing desire to pray, to seek him, to meet with him.

---

[5] Smith & Clark, © 1947, 1958 Singspiration Music/Brentwood Benson Music PublishIng/CopyCare

Matthew Henry, the 16th. century writer and minister, said - "Whenever God is about to do something truly great, he first sets his people a praying!"

Many commentators speak of a growing sense of Messianic anticipation at this time in Israel. How widespread it's difficult to gauge. Yet the principle seems clear: heightened spiritual expectations give rise to prayer, and prayer paves the way for God to act.

> *O come, O come, Emmanuel*
> *and ransom captive Israel,*
> *that mourns in lonely exile here*
> *until the Son of God appear.*
> *Rejoice, rejoice,*
> *Immanuel shall come*
> *to thee, O Israel.*[6]

Going further…

- Look back over your own life. Can you see God at work in times of apparently random happenings? Give thanks for his presence and guidance, real though often unseen.

- How can you align yourself with what God is doing in the world today?

- One key aspect of this Advent journey is sharing with others as we travel together. What do you want to share from these first few days?

---

[6] 12th. century carol, translated by John Mason Neale (1818-66)

Day 5: Read Luke 1:11-17

Angels
Living in a Western world ruled by logic and rational thought has often left little room for supernatural encounters. However, Doctor Luke's careful research into the story leaves us in no doubt that the coming of Jesus is marked by angelic appearances and miracles. God is intervening directly in daily life, as he does when Zechariah offers incense in the sanctuary. There he encounters an angel standing at the right hand side of the altar.

The standard response to dramatic angelic appearances in Scripture is fear (v12-13). This is no sudden and short-lived fright. Zechariah is truly terrified. He neither expects this, nor views it as a common occurrence. And the first angelic words on such occasions? "Do not be afraid," in this instance to be augmented by an incredible promise of a baby boy.

Prayer
What was Zechariah's prayer (v13)? His personal request for a son and heir, or his liturgical prayer for the redemption of Israel? The first seems unlikely, given the ages of this elderly couple. The second possibility could well be answered by the first. Israel's redemption would come through the Messiah. The child to be miraculously conceived by Elizabeth, and named John, would be the forerunner of the Messiah (v17). "God's answers (to prayer) sometimes come at a surprising time, in a surprising place, and in a surprising way"[7].

Joy
Luke uses some of his favourite words in v14. "Joy…delight…rejoice". These arise from experiencing the Holy Spirit making real God's saving action. The angel predicts that the miracle baby to be born will be filled with the Holy

---

[7]Darrell L. Bock, Baker Commentary on *Luke 1:1-9:50*, page 83.

Spirit even before his birth. John becomes "a precursor of God's coming ministry of the Spirit in the church, when the Spirit will be given not just to a few but to all who believe"[8].

*He shall come down like showers
upon the fruitful earth;
love, joy and hope, like flowers
spring in his path to birth:
before him, on the mountains,
shall peace the herald go,
and righteousness in fountains
from hill to valley flow.*[9]

Going further…

- What help is there in this passage for those struggling with unanswered prayers?

- Compare v17 with Malachi 4:6. John's ministry offered hope of reconciliation between family members through mutual reconciliation with God. Are there broken or strained relationships that you need to address? Let this time of Advent be a time to work towards reconciliation and healing. Pray about one step you can take, and do it!

---

[8]Bock, page 86.

[9] James Montgomery (1771-1854), v3, *Hail to the Lord's Anointed*

Day 6: Read Luke 1:18-25

Zechariah's words seem innocent at first. Either in the way they were expressed, or because of Gabriel's insight, Zechariah's unbelief is exposed, and sentence pronounced. In asking for a sign, Zechariah seems to have quickly forgotten the miracle of Gabriel's appearance in itself being a remarkable indication of God's presence. Instead he sees the difficulties in the way of fulfilment. I guess all of us know what that feels like, although mercifully few, if any, have experienced the old priest's temporary judgement.

Faith and doubt
Are there times when God silences us in order to discipline us, yet simultaneously prepare us for his great blessing? The sign Zechariah requested (v18) is granted (v20) but not in the way he expected! Zechariah is being called to believe the good news relayed by Gabriel in v13-17, and the promise God had made. He is called to faith instead of doubt.

While Zechariah is in the temple, the gathered congregation outside are waiting and wondering, maybe also worrying? Would Zechariah emerge to pray for them and bless them? When he does come out, Gabriel's first sign is fulfilled, and Zechariah is reduced to hand signals to try and communicate something of his experience (v22).

Speaking and listening
Are there times we need to stop talking and really start listening to God? Friends who have been struck down with illness have sometimes reflected that it gave them space to do just that. Zechariah must have spent many days considering his own predicament, not least when he tried to communicate Gabriel's message to his wife Elizabeth.

"God is faithful" (1 Corinthians 1:9).

The miracle happens. Elizabeth becomes pregnant, acknowledging that God has made this possible (v25). Despair and doubt give way to praise. This elderly couple have experienced first hand the promise and the power of God. We don't know why Elizabeth hides herself away for five months (v24), but the brief reaction to her pregnancy that Luke records (v25) displays a devout woman who is very conscious of God's activity in her life. His eternal purpose is being fulfilled through a baby promised to a childless couple.

Going further...

- Pray today for couples who are coping with childlessness.

- Can you recall a time when God brought you from doubt to faith? Share your story.

- "Everybody should be quick to listen, slow to speak"[10]. Take time to listen for God.

> *Into the darkness of this world,*
> *into the shadows of the night,*
> *into this loveless place you came,*
> *lightened our burdens, eased our pain*
> *and made these hearts your home.*
> *Into the darkness once again*
> *oh come, Lord Jesus, come*[11]

---

[10] James 1:19

[11] Maggi Dawn, © 1993 Thankyou Music

Day 7: Read Luke 1:26-33

Many of us will be able to think of a day that changed our lives. For Mary, it was the day the angel came. Six months after Elizabeth conceives, the angel Gabriel is given another assignment. This time he is to meet a young, engaged, but unmarried woman, and deliver news unparalleled in the history of the world. Can you imagine Mary sharing this story, carefully recalling this supernatural encounter? Her surprise indicates that she seems to be more troubled by what Gabriel says, curious and anxious rather than amazed that an angel is right there beside her! Tomorrow we will reflect on what troubled her, but today we focus on the message Gabriel brought.

An encouraging message
"You have found favour with God" (v30). Mary was almost certainly a teenager when this happened. She was engaged to Joseph, but at this time was a virgin. God's affirmation of her indicates divine knowledge and awareness of this young woman. Twice she is told that God has freely and graciously favoured her, that he is with her.

A prophetic message
"You will be with child…a son…give him the name Jesus" (v31). The promise of a baby to a young woman contrasts with the previous story of the elderly Zechariah and Elizabeth. Yet both boys are promised by God and destined for great things in his plan, especially Jesus - "Saviour".

A stunning message
"He will be called the Son of the Most High…his kingdom will never end" (v32-33). A royal baby, from the line of David, with an unending kingdom is promised to a peasant girl in rural Nazareth. Can you imagine that young woman trying to take it in? She obviously remembers what the angel said, but the enormity of it is mind-blowing.

In 1 Corinthians 1:26-31, the apostle Paul would later write about God's ways and choices. "He chose the foolish things of the world to shame the wise...he chose the weak...he chose the lowly..." This is truly counter-cultural, for we instinctively look for the powerful, the strong, the famous to get things done. God chooses the unknown teenager Mary.

And yet the focus of Luke's story shifts from Mary to her baby. The angel's words turn our attention to the child she is to conceive and bear. If we fix our attention on Mary, we will miss the thrust of the angelic message, and the wonder of Jesus. This is captured in a recent, and much recorded, Christmas song.

> *Mary, did you know, that your baby boy*
> *will one day walk on water?*
> *Mary, did you know that your baby boy*
> *would save our sons and daughters?*
> *Did you know that your baby boy*
> *has come to make you new,*
> *this child that you've delivered*
> *will soon deliver you?*[12]

Going further...

- Although specially chosen by God, Mary is not coerced but invited to respond positively, while the cost to her would be considerable. Burdens often accompany blessings, but the promise of God's presence pervades all (v28).

- Have you ever been troubled by a greeting (v29)? How did you respond, and how do you respond now to Gabriel's message to Mary?

---

[12] Buddy Greene & Mark Lowry

(Sun)Day 8 - Messianic Psalm 8

At Bible College years ago we were given good advice on handling and communicating God's Word. "Let the Bible interpret itself". One key factor in determining which psalms can be described as Messianic is how they are handled elsewhere in the Bible. The four psalms chosen for this Advent journey are all quoted in the New Testament and applied to Jesus. Two writers use Psalm 8: the apostle Paul, writing in 1 Corinthians 15:25-28, and the unknown writer of Hebrews, in chapter 2:5-8.

The section they focus on is Psalm 8:3-6. As the psalmist David celebrates the majesty of God revealed in creation, he reflects on the significant role given to human beings. To us this wonderful Creator God entrusts the care and the governance of the world he has brought into being. We are made in his image. We are given stewardship over creation itself, including all plant and animal life. We are responsible to him.

The Son of Man

"The son of man" may here primarily express someone who represents humanity entrusted with this responsibility. This phrase appears elsewhere in the Old Testament, with a growing sense of its significance. Supremely it is used by Jesus as his favourite way of describing himself, and his God-given mission. It's use in Psalm 8 is embryonic.

Only as we look back through the lenses of the New Testament and the life of Jesus do we realise how amazing is the inspiration of Scripture…

- **"You made him a little lower than the heavenly beings".** The humility demonstrated in the incarnation is staggering. In Philippians 2:8 Paul tells us about Jesus taking on human form, becoming obedient to death, even death on a cross. For his readers, that's about as low as you could ever go.

- **"You crowned him with glory and honour"**. God's way is humility before glory. But glory comes, as the self-emptying leads to divine approval and exaltation. The Son of Man who humbled himself to the manger is now crowned with glory at the Father's right hand. He is Lord.

- **"You put everything under his feet"**. In Scripture there is a tension between "now" and "not yet". All things are envisaged as under his feet, although there is a sense of "not yet". 1 Corinthians 15:24-28 picks up this theme from Psalm 8 and expounds it more fully. Jesus is Lord, and the day is coming when the full implications of that profound statement will be finally realised. Could King David ever have imagined the ramifications of the psalm he wrote in celebration of creation?

> *He humbled Himself to the manger,*
> *And even to Calvary's tree;*
> *But I am so proud and unwilling*
> *His humble disciple to be.*
>
> *He yielded His will to the Father,*
> *And chose to abide in the Light;*
> *But I prefer wrestling to resting,*
> *And try by myself to do right.*
>
> *Lord, break me, then cleanse me and fill me*
> *And keep me abiding in Thee;*
> *That fellowship may be unbroken,*
> *And Thy Name be hallowed in me*[13]

---

[13] Roy Hession, *The Calvary Road*.

Going further...

- Trace the references to "son of man" in your Bible; use an index or concordance, or do an online search.

- Reflect on what you find, and share what you learn.

Day 9: Read Luke 1:34-38

"Nothing is impossible with God"
How could Mary conceive a baby while still a virgin? Her confusion in some way mirrors Zechariah's earlier doubt (1:18). Mary's question though is about something that has never happened before in human history. How can it possibly come to pass?

"Nothing is impossible with God"
Gabriel's answer directs Mary to the Holy Spirit, who would bring to Mary the creative power of the Most High God. By his overshadowing of Mary, a new creation will take place within her womb: Christ will be formed in her. He will be the Holy One, the Son of God. Jesus comes from God.

Jesus later spoke to Nicodemus about the new birth in John 3:1-8. What seemed impossible to Nicodemus was, and is, possible through the divine work of the Holy Spirit in human beings. The apostle Paul would also talk about a new creation in 2 Corinthians 5:17; so would Peter in 1 Peter 1:23. It's a miracle, but nothing is impossible with God!

Up to that point in time, no woman had experienced what Mary is promised. Yet her experience is mirrored in every person who is born of the Spirit, in whose life is implanted the seed of Christ. Mary is the prototype. The Holy Spirit is the divine agent. The new humanity, the new creation, the new future of the world, begins with the conception and formation of Jesus as Mary's fully human son, one who is simultaneously the Holy One, the Son of God. In "The Giving Gift" Tom Smail contrasts the experience of Mary with that of all who are born again. In Smail's words, Mary becomes "a sign and promise of how through the Holy Spirit the same Christ will in a different way be formed in all Christians"[14].

---

[14]Smail, *The Giving Gift*, Holder & Stoughton, page 23

"Nothing is impossible with God"

The implications for Mary are not spelled out in the text. Yet we can vividly imagine the problems facing her. Like telling her fiancée Joseph; coping with gossip and suspicions from her family and community; potentially surviving as a single parent; providing for the baby; and so on. Her response in v38 is remarkable and inspiring. As the Lord's servant, it seems that whatever lies ahead, she is willing to entrust her future as well as her present to this God with whom nothing is impossible. The experience of Mary's relative Elizabeth (v36) is a sign for Mary of the power of God. The circumstances are different, but the same God is at work in both of these women.

Going further…"Nothing is impossible with God"

- What do you long to see, yet it seems impossible to you right now? Bring all those situations before God, and if you can, share them with others. As you pray, ponder and use Mary's words in v38.

- Give yourself to God, as Mary did, allowing the Holy Spirit to do his work.

- Rejoice in the wonder of the new creation, and in the uniqueness of Jesus, the son to be born of Mary. As you focus on him and worship him, may you see your own situation in a different light.

THE RISING SUN

Unto us a boy is born,
King of all creation,
Came he to a world forlorn,
the Lord of every nation...
...now may Mary's Son, who came
so long ago to love us,
lead us all with hearts aflame
unto the joys above us[15]

---

[15] 15th. century German carol, translated by Percy Dearmer (1867-1936)

Day 10: Read Luke 1:39-45

Our readings, although taking us slowly through Luke 1, are spread over 28 days. The events recorded were spread over a much longer period, at least one year. For the people directly involved, those special, carefully recorded moments, were interspersed with many other routine times and daily tasks. All the while they were waiting expectantly to see exactly how God's plans would come to pass. This mix of special times and daily rhythms may well resonate with our experiences of the Lord who is God in all situations.

Thus far in Advent we have read about angels, visions, and miracles as God's plan is unveiled. Now an unborn child makes his presence and feelings known with regard to another unborn child. In our world, where abortion is widely practised, the idea that unborn children can potentially experience the Holy Spirit's presence (see Luke 1:15) and respond to external stimuli is a sobering reminder of the sanctity of human life from conception onwards.

Mary and Elizabeth
Why did Mary decide, hurriedly, to go and visit Elizabeth, making a journey of 80-100 miles? Why stay for three months (see v56) until Elizabeth's pregnancy was almost complete, and then leave? Was it because of Gabriel's message (v36), an opportunity for two female relatives simply to spend time together sharing what God was doing in their lives, supporting one another? Did Mary then sense it was time to go back home?

Mary's arrival and greeting sparks some astonishing responses -

- From the baby Elizabeth is carrying: the boy who would become the man John the Baptist. The unborn child leaps in his mother's womb. John is even now beginning his ministry as the forerunner of the Messiah in responding to his presence.

- From Elizabeth herself, who at that moment is filled with the Holy Spirit and speaks out in a loud voice.

- From Elizabeth's prophetic insight. She describes Mary as "the mother of my Lord," and declares her greatly blessed, because of the child she is carrying, and because she trusted God.

Blessing and believing
In Elizabeth's closing words, the first beatitude in Luke's gospel, she states very clearly that Mary's blessing has come through believing God. In contrast to doubting Zechariah (v20), Mary's faith is clear, responding with trust to the words God has spoken to her through the angel Gabriel. In Scripture, real faith is always a response to what God has said. We are blessed through believing.

Going further…

- Take time to reflect on the hymn below (v1-2 today, v3-4 tomorrow), based on Mary's song of praise to God. Read it, pray it, sing it, and share it…

Tell out, my soul, the greatness of the Lord!
Unnumbered blessings, give my spirit voice;
tender to me the promise of His word,
in God my Saviour shall my heart rejoice.

Tell out, my soul, the greatness of His name!
Make known His might, the deeds His arm has done;
His mercy sure, from age to age the same;
His holy name, the Lord, the Mighty One[16]

---

[16] From Luke 1, Timothy Dudley-Smith, v1-2

Day 11: Read Luke 1:46-56

Below is the second part of Timothy Dudley-Smith's great hymn, using Mary's words of praise from today's Bible reading - often referred to as the "Magnificat".

Tell out, my soul, the greatness of His might!
Powers and dominions lay their glory by.
Proud hearts and stubborn wills are put to flight,
the hungry fed, the humble lifted high.

Tell out, my soul, the glories of His word!
Firm is His promise, and His mercy sure.
Tell out, my soul, the greatness of the Lord
to children's children and forevermore![17]

Mary and Hannah

For Jewish people who knew the old Testament, Mary's song of praise would remind them of Hannah's similar experience many centuries earlier. After years of infertility and desperate prayer, Hannah bore a son. Following his birth, as she came to dedicate him to the Lord's service, she spoke out her praise in 1 Samuel 2:1-10. Her son was destined to be a great prophet of the Lord and leader in Israel.

Mary's song

Although Mary would have known about Hannah, she makes this song her own. Her heart is opened up in poetic and prophetic praise to God. From deep within her own being ("my soul") she joyfully praises the God who is her Saviour. "From now on" (v48) is a significant phrase in Luke's gospel, indicating a clear development in God's plan. Once touched by God, we can never be the same.

In v51-54 Mary speaks prophetically, as if these events have already occurred. This happens elsewhere in the Bible,

---

[17] Timothy Dudley-Smith, v3-4.

indicating complete confidence that God will bring all his purposes to fruition. It's as if the speaker is looking back from a future perspective and rejoicing that God has done it. This mighty, merciful, and holy God will manifest himself to his faithful people, as he has promised from the time of Abraham.

Mary's spirit and self-awareness shines through this song. She sees herself as a humble servant (v48 & 52); a woman who fears God (v50); one who trusts in the mighty God (v51); and a recipient of grace from the Lord who cares for the hungry and poor (v53). Protestants often feel that Roman Catholics make too much of Mary; yet the opposite danger is to minimise the role of this remarkable young woman. Her song of praise opens her heart to God, and to us, displaying a woman whose example and faith we can gladly pray to imitate.

Going further...

- Consider how often God's response to the needs of His people and their earnest prayers comes through the birth of a child. Could one of the children you know have been born in answer to prayer, and be destined by God for a special purpose? Pray for our children, and all involved in their nurture and growth.

- Remember that these two special children - John and Jesus - would both die in the prime of their lives. Mary would certainly know great suffering as well as great joy; Elizabeth may not have lived to hear of her son's later execution. But what really matters to both of these women is that God's saving purpose is fulfilled.

- Read Mary's song of praise again. Which part strikes you or touches you? Share that with someone else, or in your small group.

Day 12 - Read Luke 1:57-66

Soon after Mary's departure (v56) Elizabeth's time has come, and her son is born. The joy of Elizabeth and Zechariah is shared throughout their family and community. But when it's time to circumcise the baby on the eighth day (the normal practice for Jewish boys) there is controversy over the name to be given him.

It might seem strange to us that others apart from his parents would be involved in naming the child, but this story reflects close-knit Middle Eastern families and communities.

What's in a name?
Why was it so important that the baby was called John, meaning "God is gracious"? The angel Gabriel had earlier instructed Zechariah about this (v13), and presumably Zechariah had somehow conveyed this to Elizabeth (v60) in spite of being struck mute (v20).

There's also the possibility that Zechariah was temporarily deafened. The word that describes him as being mute can imply being both deaf and mute. This may account for the gathered people signing to him to ask his opinion (v62).

Zechariah's written answer causes wonder amongst those assembled. "His name is John" (v63). Zechariah's reply displays obedience to the angel and submission to God. He has learned his lesson. Immediately he is released from his temporary loss of speech, and praises God.

Did Charles Wesley have Zechariah's experience in mind when he wrote the following words…

*Hear Him, ye deaf, His praise, ye dumb,
your loosened tongues employ:
ye blind, behold your Saviour come,
and leap, ye lame, for joy*[18]

God has shown His mercy, his loving action, to this elderly couple in the gift of a baby. It's a great time for family and neighbours to rejoice together.

A special child

Apart from the brief comment that the Lord's hand is upon this child (v66) and a summary statement about his early life (v80), the next time we read about John in Luke's gospel is when he commences his ministry, preaching in the wilderness. See Luke 3:1-6.

After listing the powerful and influential movers and shakers of his day, Luke tells us about the really significant person of that time. "The word of God came to John the son of Zechariah in the wilderness". That statement could well be a comment on Mary's song in Luke 1:52 - "He has brought down the mighty from their thrones and exalted those of humble estate".

This special child receives a special name. He is destined to be great in the sight of God. Jesus himself would later describe John as the greatest man who ever lived, up to that time (Luke 7:28). Yet John is merely the forerunner of the Messiah, preparing the way for Him.

Going further...

- Consider why it was so important that Zechariah and Elizabeth's son was called John.

---

[18] Charles Wesley (1707-88), *O for a thousand tongues to sing*

- "The hand of the Lord was with him" (v66). How can you tell when God's hand is upon someone? What should you look for?

- Think about Zechariah's experience. Having been left mute for some time, now his tongue is released to praise God again. Can you think of a time God brought you into a new place of release and praise? Share that story.

Day 13 - Read Luke 1:67-79

New songs are one manifestation of special times when God is at work. Singing God's praise allows us to express what's in our hearts. When we experience the Holy Spirit filling us, as Zechariah did (v67), the outcome can be powerful. Zechariah's hymn of praise, often referred to as the "Benedictus", like Mary's earlier hymn the "Magnificat," is prophetic as well as poetic. When the Holy Spirit inspires, senior citizens are capable of writing great hymns just as much as teenagers!

Zechariah and Elizabeth were rejoicing in the birth of their son John, overwhelmed by the mercy of God to them in their old age. Yet when the father speaks out his prophetic praise, the subject of his praise is not their son.

Zechariah's hymn
V68-75: In the first part of his hymn, Zechariah remembers God's ancient promises and redemptive plan for his covenant people. This will be brought to pass through a royal descendant of King David who will deliver God's people from their enemies.

V76-79: Now in the second part, the old priest speaks about his son's role as a prophet. Yet his real focus is on the Lord who is coming (v76) and for whom his son will prepare the way. He will bring salvation, with all that means for Zechariah and his people: "God has not abandoned covenant commitments and promises made to Israel. Salvation unites the real world with the world of the heart and the world of heaven…God's salvation…is designed to show God's greatness to all the creation…total deliverance for God's people"[19].

---

[19] Darrell L Bock, pages 176 & 179.

Prophetic praise

Parents and grandparents love to tell stories and show pictures of their children and grandchildren. There really are none to compare with their offspring, and they can talk all day about their exploits. So when you meet an old man who now has eventually and miraculously become a father, you don't really expect him to talk about anything other than his son.

That makes Zechariah's prophetic praise all the more amazing. John is and will be great. But Jesus will be infinitely greater. It's through Jesus' ministry that salvation will come, offering forgiveness, mercy, and hope to those living in darkness. Graham Kendrick's hymn captures the spirit of Zechariah's praise.

> *Darkness like a shroud covers the earth,*
> *evil like a cloud covers the people;*
> *but the Lord will rise upon you,*
> *and his glory will appear on you,*
> *nations will come to your light.*
> *Arise, shine, your light has come,*
> *the glory of the Lord has risen on you;*
> *arise, shine your light has come -*
> *Jesus the Light of the world has come*[20]

John the Baptist's relationship to Jesus is sometimes compared to the moon and the sun. John is like the moon, reflecting the sun's rays, whereas Jesus is the "rising sun" (v78) who brings light to the world. John is a prophet, but Jesus is the Son of God.

---

[20] Graham Kendrick, © 1985 Kingsway's Thankyou Music.

Going further...

- In v74-75 Zechariah speaks about being rescued in order to serve God "in holiness and righteousness". How are you serving him? What is most important as you serve?

- We may think of salvation being purely spiritual. This prophetic song seems to go much further. Explore the dimensions of salvation in Zechariah's song.

- Throughout Luke 1, there is a focus on the Lord who is coming. What effect are these daily readings having on your own preparations during Advent? Talk and pray about this in your group.

Day 14 - Read Luke 1:80

Apart from his conception and birth, this one verse is all we know about John the Baptist until his ministry begins and he appears in public to herald the coming of the Messiah. John was growing physically and spiritually. His days before embarking on his public ministry were spent in the "wilderness". This was probably the area in the Jordan valley, the barren wilderness of Judea south west of the Dead Sea. Look at its location in a Bible map.

Did Zechariah and Elizabeth die while John was growing up? Possibly - perhaps probably, given their advanced ages when he was born. For older parents there can be real concerns about what happens to their children when they are gone; yet this one verse indicates that John's development was being overseen by God. We can safely entrust to his keeping all those we love.

John was about 30 years old when he began preaching (see Luke 3:2-3). Preparation for his ministry went on throughout his young life. "The Lord's hand was with him" (v66), and if that is so, there is great hope.

Going further...

- What young people do you know and pray for regularly? If the answer is none, correct that immediately! Start praying for them to come to know God, to grow and become strong in spirit, as John was. Ask God to fulfil His purpose in their lives.

- Approximately halfway through these Advent readings, how has God been speaking to you? What can you share with others from your own readings, reflections and prayers?

- Each day in these readings there has been a quotation from an appropriate hymn or song. Choose one of your own favourite Advent hymns or songs today and take time to read carefully and prayerfully through the words.

(Sun)Day 15 - Messianic Psalm 110

This psalm is one of the most quoted Old Testament passages in the New Testament. Matthew, Mark, Luke, Paul, Peter, the unknown writer of Hebrews, and significantly Jesus himself, all refer to this psalm. Check this out in any footnotes or references in your Bible. Why is this psalm so important?

Originally it seems that the psalm highlighted the role of king in Israel, and what was required or expected of him. It may have been written as King David anticipated those who would follow him as king, most likely his son Solomon. It could have been used in coronation ceremonies.

Yet it goes far beyond any identifiable future kings of Israel, and any accomplishments they would enjoy, and foresees the Messiah. It's this that so gripped the minds and hearts of the New Testament writers, and of Jesus himself (Matthew 22:41-46) when quoting from this psalm. Jesus said that David spoke these words through the influence of the Holy Spirit. How then does this inspired psalm view the coming Messiah?

"My Lord" (v1)
Don't miss the opening words reflecting a heavenly conversation - "the Lord says to my Lord". This suggests discussion within the Godhead, while the Holy Spirit is at work inspiring and guiding David to write. Does this point us toward the Trinity, as the three divine persons collaborate?

It's Jesus who presents the Jerusalem Pharisees with a further question based on this psalm. If David speaks about the Messiah as "my Lord," how can he simultaneously be his son, or descendant? A mystery that can only be grasped through the incarnation of Jesus who is both son of David and Son of God.

Mighty King (v2-3)

The powerful dominion of this great King will extend outwards from Jerusalem, overcoming all enemies, ultimately encompassing all nations, Jews and Gentiles alike (v6). The King is accompanied by a priestly people, who find constant renewal of their life with him.

"Priest for ever" (v4)

Melchizedek is one of the most wonderful yet mysterious Old Testament characters. His sole appearance is in Genesis 14:17-20. Hebrews 7 later comments extensively on his identity, his ministry and role. A Gentile priest who also was king of Salem, he is honoured by Abraham who offers him one tenth of the spoils from his victory in battle. No mention is made of his birth or death, so in one sense his priesthood never ends. He becomes a vivid figure pointing forward to Jesus, our King and great High Priest, our "priest for ever".

Heavenly Victor (v5-7)

Luke's gospel does not mention directly the dangers faced by his family when the life of the infant Jesus is threatened. Luke will give some indication of the effect his coming will have in 1:52, 71, 74 and 2:34-35. He will go on to speak of the opposition to Jesus, his rejection and crucifixion, but also of his resurrection and ascension. The Lord's anointed Servant and Son will be victorious over all who oppose him. He is the Heavenly Victor who defeats his enemies and conquers the nations, with his head lifted up in triumph.

Going further…

- It's the doubting disciple Thomas who uses words found in this psalm when he encounters the risen Jesus. Thomas affirms him as "my Lord and my God" (John 20:28). Jesus is Lord. Can you describe him as "my Lord"?

THE RISING SUN

- Use Mavis Ford's words below for meditation, praise, and prayer as you come to worship God with his priestly people today…

*You are the King of glory,
you are the Prince of peace,
you are the Lord of heaven and earth,
you're the Son of righteousness;
angels bow down before you,
worship and adore
for you have the words of eternal life,
you are Jesus Christ the Lord.
Hosanna to the Son of David!
Hosanna to the King of kings!
Glory in the highest heaven
for Jesus the Messiah reigns!*[21]

---

[21] Mavis Ford, © 1978 Springtide/Word Music (UK)

Day 16 - Read Luke 2:1-5

God and Caesar

God is in ultimate control within our world today. We need to affirm that and live in the light of it. Just as he was in control of the events leading up to and surrounding the coming of his Son into the world. Caesar Augustus, the first Roman emperor, known for his peaceful reign, may well have been ignorant of that. So too Quirinius, the Syrian governor whose territory included Palestine. Yet through the decree issued for a census to be taken, probably for tax purposes, Mary and Joseph embark on a journey from Nazareth. In the process, God is using Augustus. Micah's prophecy is being fulfilled, predicting the birth of the Messiah in Bethlehem (see Micah 5:2). He will be the true Prince of Peace, offering peace that could never be experienced under the rule of any Roman emperor.

Luke says nothing about the angelic appearances to Joseph recorded in Matthew's gospel; Luke is telling Mary's story. And what a story, for a heavily pregnant young woman facing a trek of at least three days, covering 80-90 miles, just to be registered in the census. Nevertheless they head off, back to Joseph's ancestral home. We can only conjecture how difficult that trip must have been, especially for this young woman.

God moves...

God's control of circumstances and events may mean upheaval and discomfort for us. He "moves in a mysterious way, His wonders to perform"[22], but he does move, to accomplish his plan in complete conformity with all he has said and done in the past.

The coming of Jesus completely altered the course of life for both Mary and Joseph. Any plans they may have dreamed

---

[22] From the poem by William Cowper, writing in 1773.

about had to be drastically changed. Their future was uncertain, the detail of daily challenges like food and shelter unknown. Safety on their journey, work for Joseph, care for mother and baby, health and wellbeing for this young couple: all these everyday concerns suddenly became more real and daunting. The coming of the incarnate Lord turned their lives around.

Is it any different today? All too often we hear of the plight of refugees, forced to leave their homeland through famine, war, or work. Many will be unable to return. The incarnation of Jesus places him in the context of displaced people, ruled by forces over which they have no control. God understands. He sees. He knows. And behind the authority of the Roman emperor, the eternal God is in control.

> *And those whose journey now is hard,*
> *whose hope is burning low;*
> *who tread the rocky path of life*
> *with painful steps and slow.*
> *O listen to the news of love*
> *which makes the heavens ring,*
> *O rest beside the weary road*
> *and hear the angels sing*[23]

Going further...

- Consider the impact Jesus has had in your life. How has his coming affected you, and with what results?

- Do you follow national and international news and events? Is it possible that God is using what's going on in the world today to accomplish his purpose? If so, how should that affect the way we pray?

---

[23] E H Sears (1810-1876), v3, *It came upon a midnight clear.*

Day 17 - Read Luke 2:6-7

Meekness and majesty
Two Bible verses, that's all. The most understated birth of all time. The eternal God takes on human flesh. We call it the incarnation, arguably the greatest miracle. An event that changed the course of history, with consequences for the whole cosmos. Jesus is born and laid in a manger in the Judaean town of Bethlehem.

Oh what a mystery,
meekness and majesty,
bow down and worship,
for this is your God[24]

Most of the Christmas carols quoted in this devotional guide centre on this event, and celebrate it, probing its incredible earthiness and profound theology. "The tone of the setting of Jesus' birth matches the tone of his ministry. The great God of heaven sends the gift of salvation to humans in a serene unadorned package of simplicity"[25].

We can look back through the lenses of the years since, through the great carols that have been written, through the myriad of theology books exploring the fact that the Almighty God, in the person of his Son, humbled himself to a manger. And so we should, mixing genuine awe with heartfelt worship as we contemplate the Christ child.

Room for Jesus?
For Joseph and Mary, how different. Mystery, yes. Wonder and awe, yes. Yet so much more. Having arrived safely in Bethlehem, where will they stay? Who will help with the

---

[24] Graham Kendrick *Meekness and Majesty,* © 1986 Make Way Music/ Thankyou Music

[25] Darrell L Bock, page 107

imminent birth? Will Joseph need to act as midwife? How will they cope with all the responsibilities and trials that come with a newborn infant, so far from home? What about the health and wellbeing of mother and baby, apparently forced into quite unsanitary conditions?

Without spoiling much loved Christmas traditions, Luke says nothing about a donkey on the journey, or animals around the manger, or an innkeeper in Bethlehem. "No room…in the inn" does indicate that potential rooms or shelters were full and therefore refuge is sought elsewhere.

Luke wants us to focus on the nature and birth of this child, in a room normally reserved for animals. Here is the first throne room for the Messiah, deprived of normal comfort, although wrapped in the traditional strips of cloth used for newborn children.

> *Thou didst leave Thy throne*
> *and Thy kingly crown*
> *when Thou camest to earth for me;*
> *but in Bethlehem's home*
> *was there found no room*
> *for Thy holy nativity.*
> *O come to my heart, Lord Jesus,*
> *there is room in my heart for thee*[26]

Going further…

- Have you welcomed him into your heart? If not, why not do so now? Pray for others to acknowledge him as well.

---

[26] Emily Elizabeth Steele Elliott (1836-97)

Day 18 - Read Luke 2:8-12

Shepherds
The first people to hear of the birth of Jesus are a group of shepherds near Bethlehem. Our frequently romantic notion of shepherds is far from the reality these men would have known. Long weeks wandering in the open countryside, finding pasture for their flocks, living with daily dangers and constant challenges. This was the life of Middle Eastern shepherds, who may often have been looked down on by those in settled communities. To such a group of lowly, humble people comes the news the world has waited for millennia to hear.

Angel(s)
Initially one angel appears to announce the good news (v9), soon to be joined by a great company of other angels (v13). Like Zechariah in the temple (see 1:12), and Mary in Nazareth (1:29) the shepherds are terrified by the angelic appearance. Additionally they experience the majestic shining glory of the Lord. This further manifestation may well cause us to reflect on the unseen presence, but real involvement, of these servants and messengers of God in our world and in our lives. Compare Hebrews 2:14.

A Saviour…Christ the Lord
The shepherds and the angel have a key place in this story, but the real focus is on the baby. The stunning announcement is enhanced by the angel's identification of the newborn baby with exalted titles reserved for God alone. Furthermore, Jesus' birth "in the town of David" (v11) and as a descendant of David (2:4), fulfils ancient prophecies.

Fear is an understandable response from the startled shepherds, yet "great joy" (v10) is more appropriate given the wonderful proclamation. To affirm the truth of his announcement, the angel gives a sign. He seems to expect the shepherds to go and find out for themselves; what happens to the sheep while they are away is much less important than finding the Saviour! "With a song in its heart, heaven sent Jesus to earth"[27].

> *Joy to the world, the Lord has come,*
> *let earth receive her King.*
> *Let every heart prepare Him room,*
> *and heaven and nature sing,*
> *and heaven and nature sing,*
> *and heaven, and heaven and nature sing*[28]

Going further…

- Imagine you are one of the shepherds. Write your story of that night.

- "Saviour…Christ (Messiah)…Lord". Consider these titles for Jesus, which appear together only here in the New Testament. What does each one mean? What is the overall message and impact Luke intends by linking them?

> *Who is He, in yonder stall*
> *at whose feet the shepherds fall?*
> *'Tis the Lord O wondrous story,*
> *'tis the Lord, the King of glory;*
> *at His feet we humbly fall,*
> *crown Him, crown Him Lord of all.* [29]

---

[27] Bock, page 212.

[28] Isaac Watts (1674-1748)

[29] Benjamin Russell Hanby (1833-67)

Day 19 - Read Luke 2:13-15

Sometimes people talk about "thin places". This usually signifies special places or encounters where any dividing line between earth and heaven seems slight. Heaven breaks through and touches earth. In today's passage, heaven addresses earth about Jesus, and why His coming matters so much. For those astonished shepherds, the Bethlehem fields must have seemed like one of those "thin places".

Glory to God...peace on earth
If one angel spooked the shepherds, how must they have felt when a host of angels appeared? Yet this great heavenly company - "the armies of heaven" (New Living Translation) - has not appeared to fight but to praise God and to proclaim peace to those on whom God's favour rests. Peace is not promised to all, but to those who seek to please God by welcoming the Saviour sent from heaven. The peace he brings is deeper, lasting, made possible through him alone (see v11). He is the Prince of Peace, as the Old Testament prophet Isaiah predicted (Isaiah 9:6). "He himself is our peace" (Ephesians 2:14).

On the road to Bethlehem...
How could the shepherds stay put, given the astounding news they received in this dramatic and divine encounter? Good news is for sharing, even if it's late, dark and dangerous. Still today, the coming of Jesus is impacting lives of ordinary people, dispelling fear with joy, offering a meeting with the Saviour who is Christ the Lord. But to meet him, we may need to set off on our own journey, through the darkness, to the manger.

The coming of Jesus disrupts as well as delights. If we don't want to be disturbed, we can block him out. But if we join in the journey to Bethlehem, we will find out for ourselves the truths that have been conveyed to us. God's peace, his shalom, awaits us; all the blessings of that shalom are offered through Jesus

> *Angels from the realms of glory*
> *wing your flight o'er all the earth;*
> *heralds of creation's story,*
> *now proclaim Messiah's birth.*
> *Come and worship*
> *Christ, the new-born King*[30]

Going further…

- Have you encountered "thin places"? Where? When? What made your experience with God special for you, and what was the outcome?

- Praise (in heaven, giving glory to God) and peace (on earth) feature strongly in today's reading. Are they connected? If so, how?

---

[30] J Montgomery (1771-1854)

Day 20 - Read Luke 2:16-20

Some parents like to keep a record of significant moments in their children's lives. Pictures, certificates, items of clothing and toys can all be kept as reminders of those wonderful, special days and experiences.

Treasured memories
It was no different for Joseph and Mary, especially Mary. Twice in Luke 2, the author tells us "Mary treasured up all these things" (v19 and 51). What things? Well, the sudden appearance of an out of breath group of Bethlehem shepherds for starters! And their amazing story of the angels appearing and announcing Jesus' birth. Following that, these men had hurried to see for themselves what had happened: "they ran to the village" (NLT). They were not the gaggle of friends or family that new parents might expect. We know nothing about what happened when they arrived and actually found the child they sought; we can only speculate about that. But their arrival on the scene, and their story, was one more memory for Mary to store away in her heart (v51).

We do know the reaction of the shepherds after meeting the parents and the baby...
"They spread the word". These humble men shared their own witness to Jesus; they are understandably sometimes called the first evangelists.

"They returned, glorifying and praising God". Back to the sheep and the hills, back to the daily routines, back to their familiar lives...but could they ever be the same again? They disappear now from the story. This may have been the last Mary and Joseph ever saw of them. Yet their experience and reaction is remembered, and they model something important for us as we consider our response to these Advent stories.

*Born in the night, Mary's child,
a long way from your home.
Coming in need, Mary's child,
born in a borrowed room.*

*Clear shining light, Mary's child,
your face lights up our way;
light of the world, Mary's child,
dawn on our darkened day*[31]

Going further…changed lives?

It's fascinating to ask how this event affected the shepherds afterwards. We simply don't know. That's their story. We do know our stories, and their responses pose some pertinent questions for us…

- What lasting impact is Jesus making in our lives? Meeting Him may have been momentous. Are we still as thrilled and awestruck as when we first found Him, or rather were found by Him?

- How are we spreading the word? "All who heard it" were amazed, or astonished, at what the shepherds told them. Pray for good opportunities to tell something of your story.

- "Glorifying and praising God" (v20) is wonderful, especially after such an incredible experience. Is our praise continually rising to God in the light of what He has done through our Lord Jesus Chris

---

[31] Geoffrey Ainger © 1964 Stainer & Bell Ltd

Day 21 - Read Luke 2:21-24

Today's reading speaks of Jesus' circumcision and consecration to the Lord, and his mother's purification, all actions undertaken by his parents in accordance with their Jewish faith. We sometimes forget that Jesus was Jewish, brought up in a devout family where he would be nurtured well spiritually as well as physically.

Obedience, devotion, consecration, sacrifice
The obedience and devotion of his parents is seen in naming the child as the angel sent by God had instructed (v21), in bringing Jesus to Jerusalem to present or dedicate him to the Lord, and in making an offering required by the Jewish law. They could have left the baby in Bethlehem and made the journey to the temple on their own to offer the appointed sacrifice. What they did was above and beyond what the law actually required for a firstborn.

Following childbirth, the mother had to wait 40 days before worshipping at the Jerusalem temple, being ritually purified there and then making an offering. This last point is significant. Leviticus 12:2-8 prescribed the offerings that were acceptable. Either a lamb and a pigeon or dove, or two pigeons or doves would suffice, depending on what the family could afford. The offering brought by Mary and Joseph suggests they were unable to afford the more expensive offering, and brought what was suited to poorer people instead.

These details recorded by Luke provide further commentary on the nature of the incarnation. The truth of the self-emptying of Jesus would be stamped upon his life from his lowly beginnings right through to the end of life. He lives among the common people; he knows hardship and need. He understands everyday concerns. He identifies with the poor, yet can minister equally to the rich. He truly is God with us.

Lord Jesus Christ, You have come to us,
You are one with us, Mary's Son,
cleansing our souls from all their sin,
pouring your love and goodness in,
Jesus, our love for You we sing,
living Lord[32]

Going further...

- **Obedience, devotion, consecration, and sacrifice**. All feature in three brief verses that we can easily pass over quickly without stopping to consider properly. Obedience, devotion, consecration, and sacrifice. Which of these four words makes you pause and reflect today?

- When Jesus later read from the scroll of Isaiah in the synagogue at Nazareth, the first words he quoted were "The Spirit of the Lord is on me, for he has anointed me to preach good news to the poor" (Luke 4:18). What does "good news to the poor" look like today?

---

[32] Patrick Appleford © Josef Weinberger Ltd

(Sun)Day 22 - Messianic Psalms. Read Psalm 16

Mary and David
If we asked Mary to pick a Psalm for today, what would she choose? Psalm 16 might be a good option, written by her great ancestor David. From what we know of her, we may imagine her asking for God's protection and help (v1). He is the Lord who lives, the focus of her worship, and her security. We might hear her speaking or singing the words in v5-7, as she trusts God with her life, her baby, her marriage, and her future.

What of the author, King David? We know much about his life, but little about the precise circumstances of this psalm. We know he faced many hardships in his life, yet in his relationship with God, like Mary, he knew the wonderful security that comes from trusting in him. Living in a world of many religions, David recognises the uniqueness of the God in whom he trusts. He is the foundation of his life (v8), his ultimate goal and reward (v2). David and Mary are distanced from each other by centuries and generations, but they are kindred spirits. Each in their time expresses their absolute dependence on the living God.

The promise of life
God uses such people. Sometimes in ways that go way beyond their expectations. As Psalm 16 draws to a conclusion, it takes on a different and prophetic note, looking forward to the coming of the Messiah. Read v8-11 again; at first we understand this in the context of David's life. God, who wills life for his children, will not abandon him even to the grave in his death. Somehow, however tentatively, David looks beyond death to life with his Lord.

On the day of Pentecost, when the Holy Spirit comes upon the gathered followers of Jesus, and Peter stands among the bewildered crowd to explain what's happening, he quotes these very words from Psalm 16. See Acts 2:25-32 (and Acts

13:34-37). Peter declares that David's words, written a thousand years before Jesus, anticipate his resurrection. David "spoke of the resurrection of the Christ" (Acts 2:31).

It might seem strange to choose a Messianic psalm that anticipates the resurrection when we're in the midst of Advent. Why? This psalm celebrates life. Life under the rule of God now, life sustained through the hardships and troubles we face, and ultimately life that continues beyond death, our last great enemy. The coming of Jesus signals the gospel offer of eternal life for all who believe and follow him. "I have come that they might have life, and have it to the full" (Jesus speaking in John 10:10). All this is made possible because of the unique new life generated by the Holy Spirit in the womb of Mary.

We sometimes separate Jesus' incarnation, life, death, resurrection and ascension. All are vitally important. All express his mission and the amazing love of God revealed in him. And all are part of the one great "Christ-event" recorded in Scripture; each phase of revelation in Christ leads unbroken into the next, until the whole picture is completed by his resurrection and ascension. "Through the Spirit of holiness (Jesus) was declared to be the Son of God, by his resurrection from the dead" (Romans 1:4).

Going further...

- What is most wonderful about the life Jesus brings? Share your response with someone else today.

THE RISING SUN

Light of the world, You stepped down into darkness
opened my eyes, let me see.
Beauty that made this heart adore You
hope of a life spent with You,
so here I am to worship, here I am to bow down
here I am to say that You're my God
You're altogether lovely, altogether worthy
altogether wonderful to me[33]

---

[33] Tim Hughes

Day 23 - Read Luke 2: 25-35

Life with Jesus is never dull! Mary and Joseph would tell us that if they were alive today. During their eventful visit to the temple in Jerusalem, they encounter two devout believers who speak prophetically about Jesus. Anna was definitely an elderly lady. We don't know how old Simeon was. There are some indications that he too was well on in years; today we focus on him, followed by Anna tomorrow.

A divine encounter
For all involved, this was a truly divine encounter. For Simeon, moved by the Spirit to enter the temple precinct that very day and at that very time. For Mary and Joseph, this "chance" meeting with a complete stranger was to have a profound impact on them, long recalled by Mary in particular.

How did Simeon recognise Jesus? By the same Holy Spirit who was upon him, and had revealed to him that before he died he would see "the Lord's Christ". Inspired and guided straight to the baby, he experiences the greatest moment in his life as he takes the child in his arms and utters his famous prophecy over him. He had been waiting for the "consolation of Israel" (v25), a phrase that refers to the hope of deliverance for the nation. Simeon looked forward to the day when God completed his ancient promises.

A powerful prophecy
There are actually two prophecies shared by Simeon. The first (v29-32) is poetic, and addressed in praise to God, as Joseph and Mary listen in amazement. Simeon sees in Jesus the one who brings salvation and hope for the nations, Jews and Gentiles alike. The second prophecy (v34-35) is specifically addressed to Mary, and its accuracy in predicting the effect Jesus will have is simultaneously inspiring and disturbing.

People will be divided over Jesus. By their response to him, some will fall and some will rise: some will reject him and some will find their greatest joy through salvation in him. "And a sword will pierce your own soul too". Did Simeon's words come back to Mary at different times in her life, and especially as she stood at the cross of her beloved son some 33 years later?

*Come, Thou long-expected Jesus
born to set thy people free.
From our fears and sins release us,
let us find our rest in Thee.
Israel's strength and consolation,
hope of all the earth Thou art,
dear desire of every nation,
joy of every longing heart*[34]

Going further...

- God's timing is immaculate. Simeon could do nothing to bring about the fulfilment of the Holy Spirit's promise to him (v26). He was willing to trust God to bring this about in his time and his way. Are you trusting God like Simeon?

- Simeon could die in peace now that he had met Jesus. How many people do you know who have never yet met Jesus, nor experienced the salvation he brings? Perhaps you are one of them! Perhaps God has kept you alive until now so that you can receive Jesus and face death, when it comes, with the same hope that burned in Simeon's heart...now is the time to pray.

---

[34] Charles Wesley (1707-88)

Day 24 - Read Luke 2:36-38

During a time when I sensed God may have been preparing me for a major change in my life, I visited an elderly lady in our church who was unaware of what was happening with me. Imagine my surprise when pointedly, and with a twinkle in her eye, she invited me to talk about the prospect of moving on. God gives insight, and prophetic gifting, to old and young alike.

Anna's prophecy
The teenager Mary had many significant and memorable encounters in her young life; one more came hard on the heels of Simeon's appearance. This time an elderly lady is mentioned, her only appearance in the story of Jesus. Anna was probably between 84-105 years of age, depending on how Luke's words are translated. V36-37 can either mean she was widowed seven years after her marriage (most likely at the age of 13-14), or a widow for 84 years. This second witness to Jesus during the temple visit comes, like the first, as a real surprise, bringing further confirmation of the uniqueness of this child.

A Godly woman
Anna's character is striking. Married for only a short time, then widowed for many decades, she emerges as a woman who never succumbed to bitterness. She devoted herself to serving God, worshipping, praying and fasting. In his "Systematic Theology", Wayne Grudem says: "The work of the Holy Spirit is to manifest the active presence of God in the world, and especially in the church…he gives stronger or weaker evidence of the presence and blessing of God, according to our response to him"[35].

We see in Anna a woman whose heart is given to God, a woman so positioned spiritually that the Holy Spirit finds in

---

[35] Grudem, Systematic Theology, IVP, page 636

her someone who is ready to receive a powerful visitation. Her special moment comes when she spots Mary, Joseph, and Jesus. God's timing is precise (v38) and Anna welcomes her Redeemer. Age is no barrier to encountering God. If like Anna our hearts are genuinely open to God, he can and will meet with us through his Son.

Going further…

- "We desperately need older believers" said one young leader to me in Central Asia where the church was growing rapidly. Thank God for those who have helped you.

- What enables us to be truly open to God, like Anna, and ready to receive from him?

*What can I give to the King,
Give to the one who has everything?
What can I give, what gift can I bring?
What can I give to the King?
What can I give to the King?
Give Him a heart that's opened up wide,
give Him a life that's got nothing to hide,
give Him a love that's tender and true,
and He'll give it all back to you,
yes, He'll give it all back to you.* [36]

---

[36] Barry McGuire, © Sparrow Song/Cherry Lane Music Ltd

Day 25 - Read Luke Luke 2:39-40

Following the amazing stories surrounding Jesus' conception and birth, these two verses are all the information we have from Luke about his early life until the age of 12. Returning to Nazareth from Jerusalem, the family settle down to rural Galilean village life. No mention is made here of Matthew's story of the escape from a power-mad Herod into Egypt, and the family's sojourn there. That's another story. Luke's summary focus is on life in Nazareth for Mary, Joseph, and especially Jesus. Three brief comments are made about those childhood years.

"The child grew and became strong"
In spite of all the problems associated with Jesus' birth and post-natal life, he increases in health and strength. Care given by earthly parents is so vital at this stage in life. A hard-working, righteous father and a loving, godly mother make a great combination, providing a context for any child to flourish.

This brief comment additionally reinforces the humanity of Jesus. The Son of God comes to earth not as a fully developed man but as a small baby, facing the realities of life and human development.

"He was filled with wisdom"
Not what you would say about many children! The phrase indicates a growing awareness of God's will in the life of this child. Like John the Baptist, Jesus grows physically, but in addition he develops spiritually in the wisdom of God. Wisdom in Scripture is never nebulous or other-worldly. It is rooted in the knowledge and worship of God, and is expressed in applying God's words in the situations encountered in everyday life. Isaiah predicted that the Messiah would be called "Wonderful Counsellor" (Isaiah 9:6).

"The grace of God was upon him"

Even then? Luke's economy of words belies the incredible nature of the incarnation, as the grace of God is revealed so wonderfully in a human life. It's the apostle John who comments, "from the fulness of his grace we have all received one blessing after another…grace and truth came through Jesus Christ" (John 1:16-17). Like his mother before him, Jesus is said to live under the favour of God (see Luke 1:28 & 30).

Going further…

- We care about our children's physical growth and health. How much attention do we give to their spiritual development? Pray for children you know, and for their parents. What can you do to support and encourage children and parents alike?

> *For He is our childhood's pattern,*
> *day by day like us He grew.*
> *He was little, weak and helpless,*
> *tears and smiles like us He knew.*
> *And He feels for all our sadness,*
> *and He shares in all our gladness*[37]

---

[37] Cecil Frances Alexander, v4, *Once in royal David's city*.

Day 26 - Read Luke 2:41-48

12 years pass until we meet Jesus again. We are back in Jerusalem with him and his parents for the Feast of the Passover. This annual visit tells us a little about the upbringing Jesus had under Mary and Joseph, and their character as a couple devoted to God. Women were not required to go on this pilgrimage every year; men were. Joseph and Mary together make the yearly journey of some 80 miles to Jerusalem to celebrate the Passover, no matter how difficult or inconvenient.

Lost children
Because of frequent dangers along the way (e.g. from robbers, wild animals, and other hazards) large groups of people would often travel together up to Jerusalem. This festive and joyful occasion suddenly turns sour on the way home to Nazareth. It's every parent's worst nightmare - a missing child. If you have ever experienced this, even for a short time, consider how his mother and father must have felt as they ask around friends and family members. Jesus is nowhere to be found. They then make the return journey to Jerusalem and search fruitlessly for three days before Jesus is located. Mary's admonition of Jesus (v48) captures something of her frustration, fear and anxiety.

Lost children, alone and vulnerable in a dangerous world. Confused and frightened parents, sleep deprived and anxious. Crowds of people oblivious to the anguish as their search goes on. These last few sentences describe not only this part of Jesus' story but the grim reality of life for millions of people in our world today.

Searching questions
Jesus is found eventually. Every parent knows the mixture of relief and annoyance in that moment as emotions well up. Here he is in the Jerusalem temple, where those prophetic

words had been spoken by Simeon and Anna twelve years earlier. Now he is engaged in deep discussion with the Jewish teachers, with a hunger to listen and then respond. His words show incredible understanding and wisdom.

"Son, why have you treated us like this?" This is not the last time Mary would ask such a question. Our Scripture reading today stops here; we will read on tomorrow. Sometimes we need to live with the questions we have, bringing them before God without any guarantee of answers or satisfaction. Our anguish, heartfelt confusion and uncertainty is all part of our experience and needs to be faced, even if not willingly embraced. We should be free to ask our questions in the presence of the God who hears.

We seldom read this part of Luke's gospel during the season of Advent, and I don't know of any carols that relive the experience of Mary and Joseph. Here is true incarnation. The God of heaven is embroiled in the frantic search of parents for a missing child.

Since God is fully revealed in Jesus, God's Son, this story reminds us that he is sovereign and free. We cannot control him or what he does. There is something mysterious, yet wonderful, in the unpredictability of his divine action. In the words of Mr. Beaver, "Who said anything about safe? 'Course he isn't safe. But he's good. He's the King, I tell you"[38]. Even when we don't understand, perhaps especially when we don't understand, he is still God, and he is still present.

---

[38] C S Lewis, *The Lion, the Witch and the Wardrobe,* Collins, page 75

O what a mystery I see,
what marvellous design;
that God should come as one of us,
a Son in David's line.
Flesh of our flesh, of woman born,
our humanness He owns,
and for a world of wickedness
His guiltless blood atones[39]

Going further…

- Take time today to pray for parents who have lost children, either through death or through separation, forced or otherwise. Pray for those who work tirelessly to find those who are lost, and offer help and hope.

- Pray for the children, of whatever age, looking for home, searching for a heavenly Father who knows them and will welcome them into his loving embrace.

- Pray for the young people today who, like Jesus, have a hunger to learn God's ways. Give thanks for them, and consider how you can encourage them.

---

[39] Graham Kendrick © 1988 Make Way Music/Thankyou Music

Day 27 - Read Luke 2:49-50

Being honest with God
What do you say to a missing child who has now been found? How can you contain your anger, annoyance, frustration, and yet immense relief that the child is safe and well? You want to wrap your arms around them, and also yell at them for what they have put you through. This very human reaction seems to lie behind Mary's question and admonition (v48).

Throughout Scripture, especially in many of the Old Testament psalms, there is a very straightforward, and often quite raw, even brutal way of speaking with God. Complaints, confusion, hurt, pain, bewilderment - all of these find their place in the ancient song book of Israel. Worshippers come before God telling him what it's really like for them. Situations may or may not be resolved, but somehow in their encounter with the almighty and loving God, they come to a new place, and leave things with God.

Hearing from Jesus
Mary's words evoke from Jesus a two-fold questioning response. These are the first recorded words of Jesus. After many have spoken about him in Luke 1-2, he now speaks for himself. What he says doesn't seem to satisfy his parents (v50). Yet it adds to Mary's personal treasure chest of incidents and sayings about Jesus that would cause her much reflection in the coming years (v51).

What do his words convey to us? Whatever their intention, there are some responses we can make tentatively about Jesus at this pivotal stage in his life, the age at which it was then understood that boys were beginning to emerge into adulthood.
His self-understanding: this first record of Jesus speaking (his actual words in v49, and unrecorded discussions in v46-47) reveals his incredible knowledge and wisdom.

His unique relationship with God the Father: this relationship takes priority over all other relationships in his life, a painful fact for his parents to acknowledge.

His mission in the world: some translations read "my Father's business" instead of "my Father's house" (v49). Should his parents have understood his mission required obedience primarily to his heavenly Father?

Going further…

- If Jesus' relationship with God takes precedence over all other relationships, how does that apply to us? Is your relationship with God the priority in your life? If not, what needs to change?

- Only Jesus ever speaks about God as "my Father". He teaches his followers to say "our Father", and he reassures them that God is "your Father". Why do you think that is? What does it tell us, and how does it help us?

- Who is Jesus, and why has he come? What has Luke told us in these first two chapters? How do you answer that key question?

THE RISING SUN

*Wonderful Counsellor, Mighty God,
Father for ever, the Prince of Peace,
There'll be no end to Your rule of justice,
for it shall increase.
Light of Your face, come to pierce our darkness,
Joy of Your heart, come to chase our gloom,
Star of the morning, a new day dawning,
make our hearts Your home*[40]

---

[40] Graham Kendrick, v2 *Look to the skies there's a celebration*, © 1984 Make Way Music/Thankyou Music

Day 28 - Read Luke 2:51-52

If Jesus' action in staying behind in Jerusalem has raised issues for us, this concluding part of Luke 2 may help us. The family all return to their home and livelihood in Nazareth. Jesus is noted as being "obedient to his parents".

Living with tension
As they return to Nazareth, there may well be a growing realisation that for this family daily life will go on, but it can never really be the same. Undoubtedly a tension has arisen between Jesus' obedience to his heavenly Father, and his responsibilities to his earthly parents. As Jesus prepares to enter his teenage years, he has a real awareness of who he is and why he has come; his whole life is to be lived out of the core relationship he has with his Father in heaven. Yet he is also the son of Mary and Joseph, to whom he gives respect and obedience.

Jesus lives, grows and flourishes within that tension, or conflict. The Son of God is also the son of Mary and Joseph. New Christians who have no other believers in their immediate family will perhaps be able to grasp something of that tension. One of my friends was telling the story years ago of how his wife became a Christian before him, and then had meetings every day with her "other man," Jesus! The husband's unease calmed when he too became a believer. It's great when that happens. For many, however, the ongoing reality is living with that tension of our core relationship with God alongside our relationships with others close to us. Jesus knows what that is like, and he can help us.

And Jesus grew...
His rounded development echoes Luke's comment on John the Baptist (see 1:80), but Jesus is superior. Whereas John

"became strong in spirit", Jesus "grew in wisdom and stature, and in favour with God and man" (v52).
His uniqueness is shared not to shame or diminish us who may feel slight by comparison with him. We can never emulate him. Yet Luke seeks to help us acknowledge him as the Son of God, and to see that we too can grow in grace, as he did, with God's help.

Going further...

- Jesus lives submissively at home in Nazareth for the next 17-18 years. He accepts this, even in light of his great mission. Why do we find it hard to submit?

- "Teenager" is historically a fairly recent term. It has become synonymous with rebellion, hormones, assertions of independence, personal choices (usually the wrong ones!), and rejection of authority. If you are reading this as a teenager, and a follower of Jesus, how does his example affect you and direct you?

- How does this story help you to pray for the young people you know who are seeking to follow Jesus?

*Christ by highest heaven adored,
Christ the everlasting Lord;
late in time behold Him come,
offspring of a virgin's womb.
Veiled in flesh the Godhead see,
hail the incarnate deity!
Pleased as man with man to dwell,
Jesus our Emmanuel.
Hark, the herald angels sing,
glory to the new-born King*[41]

---

[41] Charles Wesley (1707-88)

The end - or the beginning?

We have reached the end of our Advent journey. There is so much more to explore and appreciate in the gospel of Luke. Let me encourage you to go on reading about Jesus and his mission. Luke takes it through from this point onwards into the story of the church found in the book of Acts. He shows what an incredible impact Jesus has made upon our world, and is still making today through his disciples and his church. In his coming, the long Advent wait was fulfilled.

The story goes on!

Printed in Great Britain
by Amazon